THE ISABELLA BREVIARY

Janet Backhouse

THE BRITISH LIBRARY

PUBLISHER'S NOTE
All illustrations are reproduced actual size, except for the following, which are reduced in size: figs 3, 4, 5, 6, 8, 9, 12, 13, 17, 18, 20, 21, 31, 64.

Front cover: Detail of fig. 22.

Back cover: Border decoration (f. 431 detail).

Half-title vignette: Ash Wednesday ceremony (f. 69*v* detail).

Frontispiece: St Luke at work in his painter's studio (f. 473 detail, enlarged).

Title page: Calendar decoration for January (f. 1*v* detail).

First published 1993 by
The British Library, Great Russell Street,
London WC1B 3DG

British Library Cataloguing in Publication Data
is available from The British Library

ISBN 0-7123-0269-7

Photography by Peter Carey

Designed by James Shurmer

Typeset in Linotron 300 Bembo
by Bexhill Phototypesetters, Bexhill-on-Sea

Printed in England by Balding + Mansell,
Wisbech

THE ISABELLA BREVIARY

morem tuum nos mise
ricorditer per scōrum tu
orum exempla restaura
Per.
Sci luce euāgel'. oro
nteruenIat
pro nobis qs
domine scō

THE ISABELLA BREVIARY

The Isabella Breviary is one of the gems of the British Library's vast collection of illuminated manuscripts, reflecting both the artistic and the political history of its day. It was written and illuminated in Flanders, probably at Bruges, during the last decade of the 15th century and several of the foremost craftsmen of the period contributed to its lavish decoration. Its owner, Queen Isabella of Castile, was one of the most influential figures in Europe, though today she is most widely remembered for her patronage of Christopher Columbus's first momentous voyage to the Americas in 1492. The manuscript was presented to her in or shortly before 1497 to commemorate the marriages of two of her children to the son and daughter of Maximilian of Austria, King of the Romans and his first wife, Duchess Mary of Burgundy. The first of these marriages gave her, in the person of the future Emperor Charles V, a grandson who was to unite under his rule not only the greater part of Europe but also the immensely rich territories of the New World.

Isabella died in 1504. What became of the Breviary during the ensuing three centuries is not recorded, but at the beginning of the 19th century it surfaced in England in the collection of John Dent, bibliophile, banker and Member of Parliament. According to the German art historian Gustav Waagen, who noticed the manuscript in his *Art and Artists in England* (1838), it had been removed from the Escorial during the French invasion of Spain. This is quite likely, for the Spanish royal foundation, to which many of Isabella's books were transferred by her great-grandson Philip II, was plundered by French troops in 1808 and its library suffered further losses while temporarily housed in Madrid in 1809. The Breviary has not, however, been traced among the recorded books of the Escorial, though as a service book rather than a literary or scholarly text it is unlikely to have featured in a library catalogue.

Once in England the manuscript quickly became known to bibliophiles by way of a long and ecstatic description in Thomas Frognall Dibdin's *Bibliographical Decameron; or, Ten Days Pleasant Discourse upon Illuminated Manuscripts,* published in 1817. Its subsequent history is documented in detail. At Dent's sale in 1827 it was purchased for the substantial sum of £378 by Philip Hurd Esq. of Kentish Town (and not, as commonly stated, by the better-known collector, Philip Hanrott). When Hurd's library was sold up in 1832, after his death, it changed hands again at £520. According to a note added to the relevant sale catalogue by Sir Frederic Madden, who joined the staff of the Department of Manuscripts at the British Museum in 1828 and was Keeper from 1837 until 1866, the buyer was Sir John Soane, who afterwards transferred the book to Sir John Tobin, a former Lord Mayor of Liverpool, upon payment of an additional £125. Tobin owned an outstanding group of illuminated manuscripts of a kind particularly attractive to early 19th-century taste and Madden was privileged to inspect them for himself in the summer of 1835. They included, alongside the Isabella Breviary, the very famous Bedford Book

1 The arms of Ferdinand and Isabella with (*left*) the arms of the Infante John and his bride, Margaret of Austria, and (*right*) the arms of Philip of Austria, Duke of Burgundy, and the Infanta Joanna (f.436*v*).

2 The Coronation of the Virgin. The arms of Francisco de Rojas appear at the foot of the page, with his dedicatory inscription to the right (f.437).

of Hours, a small Flemish Hours made for Isabella's daughter, 'Joanna the Mad' (fig. 5), and a further Hours originally designed for Francis I of France. In 1838 the entire group, by this time comprising eight volumes, was made over to Tobin's son, the Revd John Tobin of Liscard in Cheshire.

Sir John Tobin died in February 1851. At the very beginning of the following year a London book dealer, William Boone, visited the Revd Tobin and persuaded him to part with the manuscripts, which he then offered first to Lord Ashburnham and subsequently to the Trustees of the British Museum. Madden jibbed at the asking price of £3000 but to his surprise the Trustees, somewhat uncharacteristically, insisted that the purchase should be made regardless of the cost and, after some fruitless efforts to reduce the sum, the Tobin manuscripts passed into the national collection. It was more than a year later that Madden learned from Tobin himself that Boone had paid only £1900 for the whole group, at the same time persuading the vendor not to consider offering it direct to the Museum by giving '. . . . as from his own experience, such a representation of the vexatious delay, and illiberality I should certainly meet with . . . [that] I was induced to abandon my cherished intention.'

Madden's fury at Boone's duplicity was understandably very great. Nevertheless this transaction in fact ranks as one of the most significant purchases of illuminated books in the entire history of the British Museum and Library. Along with the Bedford Hours, the Isabella Breviary (now Additional MS 18851) has been recognised as one of the major treasures of the manuscript collections from the day of its acquisition. However, although it is cited in all the many publications which cover the history of 15th-century Flemish book painting, it comes as something of a shock to realise that it has been remarkably little studied solely in its own right.

QUEEN ISABELLA OF CASTILE

The royal owner of the Breviary was born in April 1451, the only daughter of King John II of Castile. Her father died when she was only three years old and was succeeded by her half-brother, Henry IV. In 1468 the death of her younger brother Alfonso placed her in direct line of succession to the throne. She thus became a very great and desirable political marriage prize, sought after by members of royal houses throughout Europe, including those of England and France. She herself favoured an alliance with her cousin Ferdinand, heir to King John II of the neighbouring kingdom of Aragon. In defiance of strong opposition from her ruling half-brother Henry, she contrived to be married to him in the autumn of 1469 at Valladolid. When Henry died childless at the end of 1474,

(Opposite page, top, left and right) 3 Double portrait of Philip the Fair and his sister, Margaret of Austria. The coats-of-arms represent the multiple territories controlled by their parents, Maximilian and Mary (National Gallery, London).

(Opposite page, bottom left) 4 Opening page of a copy of the marriage treaty of 1495 (Archivo General de Simancas).

(Opposite page, bottom right) 5 The Infanta Joanna supported by her patron saints, John the Baptist and John the Evangelist. Her arms and those of her husband, Philip the Fair, together with their linked initials, fill the margins (British Library Additional MS 18852, f.26).

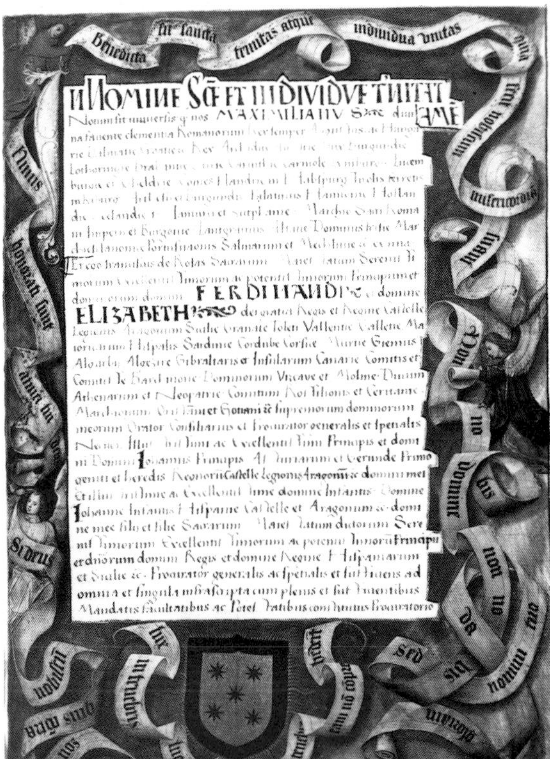
Benedicta sit sancta trinitas atque indiuidua unitas
FERDINANDI
ELIZABETH

QVI·VOVLDRA
Domine labia mea
QVI·VOVLDRA
TELE·VEVS

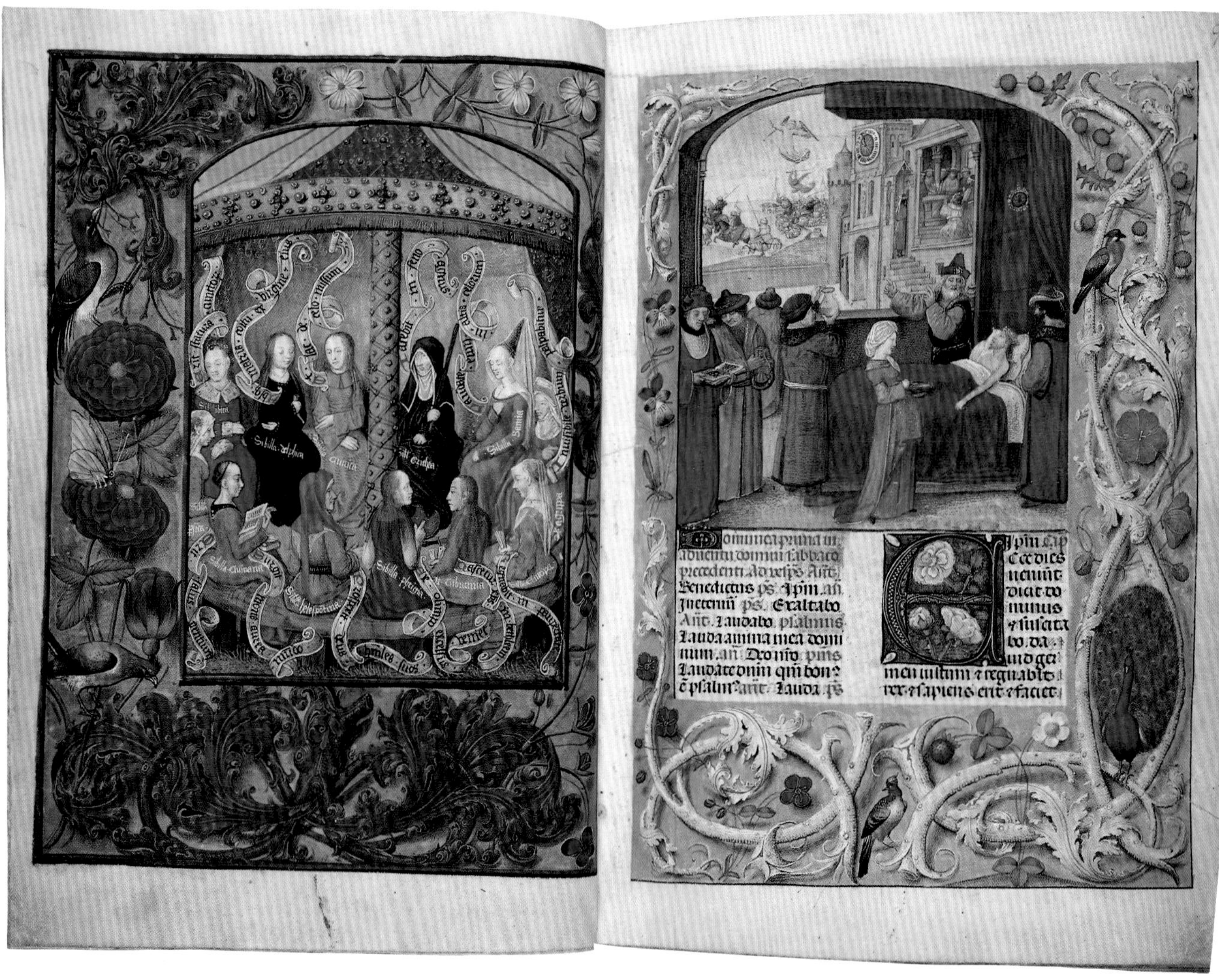

6 Advent I: twelve Sibyls foretell the coming of Christ (*left*) and (*right*) Christ's ancestor, King David, on his deathbed recalls how he built the first altar on the site of the Temple, after God had spared Jerusalem from the pestilence sent to punish his own sin of pride; Kings II. xxiv, 15–25 (ff. 8*v*–9).

Isabella proclaimed herself Queen of Castile. After a long and bitter struggle with a much younger half-sister, Joanna, whose legitimacy was in doubt but who was supported by the powerful King Alfonso V of Portugal, her right to the throne was formally acknowledged in 1479. Earlier in that same year Ferdinand's father had died, leaving him King of Aragon and Sicily, so the greater part of the area which today constitutes modern Spain came together under their rule, while remaining two independent kingdoms.

From the beginning of their joint rule, Ferdinand and Isabella took firm measures to counteract the internal disorders which they inherited from their predecessors. Among their innovations was the introduction of the Inquisition, designed to ensure the purity of the Christian faith throughout their realms. This was run by the Dominican Order and, from 1483, was directed by Friar Thomas de Torquemada, a particularly close adviser to Isabella, who had been her personal confessor before her accession to the throne. Under its auspices those Jews who refused to accept conversion were expelled from the kingdom in 1492.

7 Christmas: the Nativity (f.29).

The most resounding achievement of the joint monarchs, later granted by the papacy the complimentary title of 'Los Reyes Católicos' ('The Catholic Monarchs'), was the conquest of the Moorish Kingdom of Granada, the last stronghold of Islam in the Iberian peninsula after eight centuries of occupation. The struggle to contain the threat of Islam was a very real issue in 15th-century Europe. Constantinople had fallen to the Turks as recently as 1453. The capture of Granada by the crusading army of Ferdinand and Isabella on 2 January 1492 was applauded throughout the Christian world. (In London a service of thanksgiving was held in St Paul's cathedral.) From that moment the pomegranate badge of Granada was added to their joint royal arms, providing a useful guide to the date of many works carried out to their order. With few exceptions the dispossessed Moorish population, like the Spanish Jews, chose to go into exile, very few remaining to profess the Christian faith.

There can be no doubt of Isabella's personal devotion to the Christian religion nor of the energy with which she pursued the crusade against the Moors, riding out in person with her troops in the field. The campaign did however offer great political advantages which she and her husband were not slow to recognise, including the provision of a common enemy against whom the many diverse factions in their two kingdoms could find themselves united.

It was also in 1492, only a few weeks after the fall of Granada, that the rulers of Spain found themselves in a position to give financial support to the Genoese explorer, Christopher Columbus, for his projected voyage to the Indies. Columbus had been known to Isabella for some years and had assiduously solicited her favour, as he had that of a number of other European rulers. In her eyes one of the major attractions of his plan was the exciting opportunity which it offered to extend the Christian message to areas of the world as yet unknown. The long-term advantage to Spain of direct access to the wealth of the New World was to be fully realised only in the future. As history now records, a new continent was sighted by the expedition on 12 October 1492 and Columbus personally brought news of his discovery to Ferdinand and Isabella in their court at Barcelona in the April of the following year. He brought back with him a group of native Indians, symbolically ready to receive Christian baptism.

The early 1490s thus saw Ferdinand and Isabella fully established in their respective kingdoms, honoured for their successful and unwavering support of the catholic church, and already involved in the initial movement towards exploitation of the New World. The arrangement of suitable marriages for their five children within the framework of contemporary European politics now played a major role in their policies and it is against this background that the Isabella Breviary was produced.

THE DOUBLE MARRIAGE

The Breviary was apparently given to Isabella by her ambassador, Francisco de Rojas, to mark the marriages of her only son and direct heir, the Infante John of Asturias, and her second daughter, the Infanta Joanna (afterwards nicknamed 'the Mad'), to Margaret and Philip, the two children of Maximilian of Austria, King of the Romans, and his first wife, Duchess Mary of Burgundy. Evidence of her ownership appears in the later part

(*Left*) 8 The Circumcision (f.37). (*Right*) 9 Epiphany: the Adoration of the Magi (f.41).

of the manuscript (figs 1 and 2), where the relevant coats-of-arms and a dedicatory inscription are added. An alliance between Joanna of Castile and Philip of Austria had originally been proposed as early as 1488. At the same time embassies were also exchanged with England to arrange a contract between the youngest Infanta, two-year-old Katharine of Aragon, and Prince Arthur, the son and heir who had been born to the new Tudor King Henry VII in the autumn of 1486. Nearer to home, the eldest Infanta, Isabella, was married in 1490 to the young Crown Prince of neighbouring Portugal but was left a widow in less than a year. The Austro-Burgundian marriage plans, reactivated in 1492, were to form part of a wider political alignment against King Charles VIII of France, whose ambitions towards the Kingdom of Naples threatened Ferdinand's interests in Sicily.

Margaret of Austria's inclusion in the new negotiations made a very strong political point. In June 1483, when she was only three, she had been formally married to Charles of France, who succeeded to the French throne in that same summer. Thereafter accorded all the honours due to her rank as Queen of France, she had been brought up and very

10 Septuagesima Sunday: the Creation (f.63).

11 Lent I: the Temptations of Christ; Matthew IV, 1–11 (f.71).

(*Left*) 12 Lent III: Christ casts out a dumb devil; Luke XI, 14 (f.81*v*).

(*Right*) 13 Lent IV: Christ and the woman taken in adultery; John VIII, 3–11 (f.86).

well educated at Amboise, along with other young members of the French royal family. In 1491 she suddenly found herself repudiated in order that Charles might marry the new young Duchess Anne of Brittany, whose substantial lands to the west of France would thus be added to the kingdom. To complicate matters further, Anne herself had already gone through a proxy marriage with Margaret's father, Maximilian. Hostilities at once broke out between Charles and Maximilian and, in spite of her severed marriage, Margaret was held in France until 1493, when she was finally allowed to return to Flanders.

Francisco de Rojas, who had already represented the interests of his sovereigns in Rome and at the ducal court of Brittany, was chosen to negotiate on their behalf with Maximilian. He came of a distinguished Castilian family, an earlier member of which had been Archbishop of Toledo at the beginning of the 15th century. The safe-conduct for his journey to Maximilian's court, which he received from Ferdinand and Isabella in Barcelona at the beginning of November 1493, has survived. After discussions lasting many months, he signed the marriage contracts in their names on 20 January 1495 and represented the Spanish prince and princess at proxy weddings in the following November. In late August 1496 Joanna sailed from Spain to meet her bridegroom. After an extremely stormy and dangerous voyage, during which part of the fleet was lost and she was driven to take refuge on the English coast within the shelter of Portland Bill, she landed in Flanders and was married amidst the most splendid celebrations in the newly-built church of St Gummar at Lierre, near Malines, on 20 October. The Spanish fleet which had escorted her, duly re-fitted, set off again for Spain carrying Margaret and her retinue. This second voyage was if anything even more stormy than the first. At the beginning of February the ships were forced to put in to Southampton, where Margaret received a personal letter from Henry VII, bidding her welcome to his shores. A month later she arrived safely in Spain, where her marriage to the Infante was duly solemnised at Burgos on 3 April, Palm Sunday. The young couple were however destined to enjoy only six months together before John fell victim to a fever and died at Salamanca on 4 October. Shortly afterwards Margaret gave birth to a stillborn child, ending all hopes of securing the succession in the line of Ferdinand and Isabella's only son. The princess had greatly endeared herself both to the Spanish peoples and to their rulers during her short time as the wife of the heir to the throne. She remained at court as a beloved daughter for the better part of two years, devoting a part of her time to speaking French with twelve-year-old Katharine, soon to be sent to her own marriage in England. In later years, as Regent of the Netherlands, Margaret of Austria was to play a significant part in European politics and was also a formative influence upon her nephew Charles, the future Emperor, son of her brother Philip and his Spanish wife, Joanna.

MARKS OF OWNERSHIP

Isabella is firmly connected with the Breviary by the decoration of a single double-page opening well towards the end of the manuscript (figs 1 and 2), where a full-page display of the arms of Ferdinand and Isabella, accompanied by the arms of the two young couples, is placed opposite the arms of Francisco de Rojas and a dedicatory inscription. The de Rojas arms and the inscription are visibly painted over border decoration which had already been completed. The Spanish armorial display is on a separate leaf of vellum added to the main structure of the book. The original page bears a miniature of the Coronation of the Virgin and the juxtaposition was probably intended to convey a delicate compliment to the ruling queen by associating her with the Queen of Heaven.

The principal coat-of-arms, supported from behind by the figure of a large eagle, symbol of St John the Evangelist, and surmounted by a crown, is that normally borne jointly by the Catholic Monarchs and lavishly displayed in the decoration of the many buildings for which they were responsible. The first and fourth quarters of the shield are occupied by the quartered castles and lions which represent Castile and Leon for Isabella. In the second and third quarters the arms of Aragon impaling Sicily appear for Ferdinand. The pomegranate badge of Granada, adopted in 1492, occupies the point of the shield. A very similar armorial page, but with personal badges in place of the arms of the brides and bridegrooms, is added to a magnificent Flemish Book of Hours now in the Cleveland

14 Passion Sunday: the Jews threaten to stone Christ for blasphemy in Solomon's porch at the Temple; John x, 23–29 (f.90).

15 Palm Sunday: the Entry into Jerusalem (f.96).

16 Maundy Thursday: the Last Supper, showing Christ offering the sop to Judas, his betrayer (f. 100).

17 Good Friday: four scenes from the story of the Passion (ff. 102*v*–103).

Museum of Art. This too may possibly have originated with de Rojas. Full-page displays of the royal arms are also featured in a number of early printed books from Spain. Below are the arms of the Infante John and Margaret of Austria (*left*) and of Philip of Austria and the Infanta Joanna (*right*), the latter surmounted by the coronet of an Austrian Archduke. In each case the Spanish royal arms are combined in appropriate sequence with the arms of children of Maximilian and Mary, incorporating elements from the heraldic charges of Austria and Burgundy.

The scrolls on this page carry suitable extracts from the Psalms. That which flanks the head of the eagle reads: 'Sub umbra alarum tuarum protege nos' (Psalm 16, v.8: 'Protect us under the shadow of thy wings'). This is also used on the armorial page of the Book of Hours in Cleveland. The scrolls flanking the arms of John and Margaret read: 'Pro patribus tuis nati sunt tibi filii; constituisti eos principes super omnem terram' (Psalm 44, v.17: 'In place of your fathers your sons are born unto you; you shall make them princes over all the earth'). To the right of the arms of Philip and Joanna we read: 'Potens

18 Psalm 1: (*left*) Nebuchadnezzar presides over the burning of books at the destruction of Jerusalem; (*right*) Jerusalem is rebuilt under Nehemiah and its laws are restored by Esdras (ff. 111*v*–112).

in terra erit semen eorum; generatio rectorum benedicetur' (Psalm 111, v.2: 'Their seed shall be mighty upon the earth; the generation of the righteous shall be blessed'). Both quotations are also to be found among the biblical extracts included in the decoration of a richly illuminated copy of the marriage treaty which is now in the archives of the Dukes of Alba. This document, in book form, was illuminated in Flanders to the order of Francisco de Rojas. A second, slightly less elaborate copy, is preserved in the Spanish General Archives at Simancas (fig.4).

The arms of de Rojas himself, or five mullets of eight points azure within a bordure chequy of argent and azure, is placed in the lower margin of the right-hand page below the miniature. It is surrounded by rays of gold and flanked by scrolls bearing the words: 'Lux in tenebris lucet et tenebrae eam non comprehenderunt' (John I, 5: 'The light shineth in the darkness and the darkness overcame it not'). These arms appear in precisely the same form in both the illuminated copies of the marriage treaty.

19 Psalm 26: the coronation of David as King of Israel (f. 124).

The dedicatory inscription offering the manuscript to Isabella is written in gold letters on a brownish-purple panel, awkwardly placed in the lower part of the right-hand lateral margin of the same page. It is not at all well executed and may indeed be the work of an amateur hand. Careful scrutiny reveals that it is in fact overwritten. Underlying the text now visible is an earlier attempt to insert the same words. The spacing was so badly estimated that it would clearly have been impossible to cram the entire inscription into the available area, so the scribe painted it out and started again. Accurate interpretation of these lines, which are at one point quite badly damaged, has always proved difficult and some scholars have doubted the inscription altogether, suggesting that it is an addition made after Isabella's death, perhaps even as late as the 19th century. It has been

20 Psalm 38: David cursed by Shimei (f. 132).

pointed out that to refer to her as 'Hispaniarum et Siscilie Regine' (lines 2 and 3) is historically inaccurate as, under her own marriage treaty, she was Queen Regnant only of Castile and its associated territories, the Aragonese lands (including Sicily) being the domain of her husband. It can of course quite properly be argued that she was Queen Consort of the Aragonese realm. However, there are clear precedents to justify this particular description of her. Where the marriage treaty texts of 1495 first refer to Ferdinand and Isabella, a complete list of their territorial possessions some eight lines long appears. They are later refered to jointly in the phrase 'regis et regine hispaniarum et sicilie'. This de Rojas has gone on to apply to Isabella alone.

The damage to the lowest three lines of the inscription has resulted in some very

21 Psalm 52: Antiochus and his followers plundering the Temple (f. 139).

22 Psalm 68: David and the Temple singers, carrying allegorical flowers, beneath visions of the Passion, the sufferings of the martyrs and the destruction of Jerusalem (f. 146*v*).

23 Psalm 80: David, with a crowd of musicians, saluting the tablets of the law within the Temple, which was traditionally built on the site of the Sacrifice of Isaac, seen in the background (f. 155*v*).

curious transcriptions and explanations. In 1817 Dibdin declined to offer more than: 'H[ic] . . . marin . . . Hi ex obsequio obtulit', not wishing to 'shew the folly of an awkward attempt at its restoration'. His incomplete reading has been reproduced even as recently as 1983. When the Breviary was sold out of Dent's library in 1827 the cataloguer wrote: 'Admonished by [Dibdin's] observation, I will not make the "awkward attempt" to restore by conjecture the exact words which are defaced, but I think it may safely be affirmed that they conveyed a compliment to Isabella's patronage of Columbus's expedition. . . . . The mutilated words "H . . . . . . marin . . . . . ." furnish the Key. The Hiatus may probably be filled up nearly thus "H[is] [trans]marin [Ex] [F]". That is, "Hispaniae Transmarinae Expeditionis Fautrici ex obsequio obtulit".' This wonderfully imaginative interpretation attracted the attention of the young Frederic Madden. When the manuscript was again offered for sale after the death of Philip Hurd, he went down to Evans's sale rooms to examine it for himself. His conclusions, which are recorded both in the entry for 30 March 1832 in his unpublished diary in the Bodleian Library and in marginal notes in copies of the Dent and Hurd sale catalogues in the British Library, have apparently escaped notice until now. He experienced no difficulty in arriving at a simple and sensible reading of the key words as: 'breuiarium hoc', giving a perfectly straightforward, if somewhat over-obsequious, message.

The dedicatory inscription addressed to Isabella by de Rojas, with its abbreviations expanded, thus reads: 'Diue Elizabeth hispaniarum et siscilie Regine etc christianissime potentissime semper auguste supreme Domine sue clementissime franciscus de Roias eiusdem maiestatis humilimus seruus ac creatura optime de se merens breuiarium hoc ex obsequio obtulit.' This may be rendered as: 'To the blessed Elizabeth, queen of the Spains and of Sicily etc, his most christian, most powerful, ever august and most clement supreme lady, Francisco de Rojas, the most humble servant and creature of that same majesty, deserving of the best, of his duty offered this breviary.'

THE CONTENTS OF THE MANUSCRIPT

A Breviary contains all the material necessary for the recitation of the eight services which make up the daily Office – Matins, Lauds, Prime, Terce, Sext, None, Vespers and Compline – which constitutes the routine pattern of worship of the regular clergy. The contents varies according to the liturgical seasons and may also reflect local usage. It is frequently possible to pinpoint the area of origin of an individual book through its inclusion of the feastdays of unusual local saints. The Isabella Breviary is however a breviary of Dominican use and this offers no indications of local origin, because the liturgical practices of the Dominican Order were laid down centrally by decisions of its General Chapter and universally observed. Saints representative of all countries were selected for inclusion in the Dominican calendar, so the appearance of such figures as the English St Edward the Confessor (fig. 64) or the Bohemian St Procopius (fig. 55) has no local significance here.

The contents of the Isabella Breviary falls into several sections. It begins with a calendar (ff. 1*v*–7), in which the relevant feastdays are recorded with an indication of the level at which each is to be celebrated. This is followed by the Temporale (the Proper of the

Season) from the beginning of Advent to the Saturday in Holy Week (ff.9–110*v*). The psalter comes next, with rubrics indicating when each psalm is to be used, followed by the canticles, gradual psalms, creed and litany (ff.111*v*–200). An 11-page rubric then gives instructions for readings from the gospels according to the seasons (ff.203–208). The Temporale resumes with Easter and continues to the end of the liturgical year, with the office for the anniversary of the dedication of a church as a postscript (ff.211–292*v*). The Sanctorale (the Proper of Saints) follows (ff.293–498) and the manuscript ends with the common of saints and the commendation of souls (ff.499–525).

The decorative scheme of the book is dictated by the textual content and is designed to underline the relative importance of its various elements. Richly illuminated breviaries are far less common than richly decorated books of hours, which follow the same pattern of services in a simplified form and without seasonal variations and are specifically designed for the private use of the individual. The breviary is the working tool of the regular clergy and of members of monastic orders and as such is commonly without illumination of any kind. Luxury specimens such as the Isabella Breviary might however be ordered by wealthy but devout patrons, laymen as well as clergy, perhaps for use within a personal chapel.

In this particular manuscript virtually every page includes some kind of painted decoration, ranging from minor panels associated with the small initials introducing individual passages of text to magnificent miniatures filling some two-thirds of a page and surrounded by full borders. Although each is in itself quite simple in design, the panels which accompany minor initials exemplify the full range of border decoration fashionable in Flanders at the period when the book was made. Both compositions of coloured acanthus leaves and flower sprays set against grounds of plain vellum and panels of illusionistic flowers and fruit on gold or colour are employed. The former, typical of an earlier age and indeed rather old-fashioned in the context of the 1490s, are sometimes carried out in shades of grey alone. Where a larger initial marks a major textual division, a three-quarter border usually appears. These too include examples of both types of decoration and are mostly to be found in the early part of the manuscript, in the seasons of Advent and Christmas. With only a very few exceptions, all pages carrying a miniature, whether large or small, are given full borders. The vast majority of these are of the up-to-date illusionistic type, but examples of the older style may be seen accompanying the large miniature for Trinity Sunday (fig.38) and small miniatures from the Passion cycle (fig.17) and at the beginning of the Gradual Psalms (fig.31).

The breviary, with its extensive variety of texts, offered its illuminators opportunities to include a wide range of pictorial subjects, far less restrictive than the fairly standard cycles required for the decoration of a book of hours. In Isabella's book many of the main feasts in the Temporale are marked, predictably, by illustrations of the events commemorated, such as the Nativity (fig.7) or the Resurrection (fig.36). Others have miniatures inspired by the scriptural readings for the day, such as the miracle scenes for the Sundays in Lent (figs 12–14). In the Sanctorale the relevant saints are portrayed (fig.44 onwards). The Psalter offered particularly wide scope for illustration, since no specific events are described in the text. Scenes from the life of David were of course much favoured, but here there is a particular emphasis on the building, destruction and

24 Psalm 95: David introduces his singers of the 'old song' of the Old Testament to the 'new song' of the angels saluting the birth of Christ (f. 164).

25 Psalm 109: Abraham rescuing his nephew Lot from the enemies who had carried him off and, subsequently, greeted by the priest Melchisedek with bread and wine (f. 173).

rebuilding of Jerusalem and its Temple (figs 18, 21, 31) and on celebratory scenes of singers and musicians under David's direction (figs 22–24). There is no directly parallel cycle in any other contemporary book.

Most of the large miniatures from the Isabella Breviary are reproduced here, with a selection of the smaller ones. Those which are not included are listed below, pp.60–61.

THE ARTISTS

Several different hands participated in the decoration of the Isabella Breviary. The largest contribution is associated with an anonymous illuminator known as the Master of the Dresden Prayerbook from the book of hours in the Dresden Landesbibliothek through which his work first attracted attention. His style dominates the bulk of the manuscript, from the beginning of the Temporale (fig.6) to the feast of St Vincent Ferrer (fig.51) and thus takes in the majority of the larger miniatures, including the Old Testament miniatures in the Psalter section. The final miniature, introducing the Common of Saints, also belongs to this group, though as it is part of a discrete section it need not necessarily have been the last illustration to be painted. The style of its border decoration seems to suggest a relationship with the quire carrying the rubric concerning gospel readings, which comes before the second part of the Temporale. The Master of the Dresden Prayerbook was a very fine narrative painter, injecting much lively action into his scenes. His bystanders are as carefully characterised as his central figures and he is particularly skilled in depicting telling gestures and expressive faces to underline the significance of the main event in each of his episodes. He was also clearly fascinated by the challenge of representing figures from unusual angles and back views appear quite frequently in

(*Left*) 26 Psalm 113: Pharaoh's soldiers overwhelmed by the Red Sea after it had parted for Moses and the Israelites (f.174 detail).

(*Right*) 27 Psalm 53 (at Prime, followed by Psalm 118): ?a Ziphite messenger reveals David's whereabouts to Saul (f.176 detail).

his compositions. As this craftsman has not been identified with any of the artists of the day whose names have been recorded, it is not possible to examine his personal background. There does seem to be a Dutch flavour to his work, but there is also reason to believe that he worked for a time in Amiens. Willem Vrelant and Philippe de Mazerolles, both active in Bruges in the third quarter of the 15th century, have been named as possible influences in the formation of his mature style.

A large number of manuscripts have been associated with the Master of the Dresden Prayerbook. He seems to have worked in Bruges from about 1470 until the end of the century. He contributed mainly to books of hours and an especially fine example of his style is Additional MS 17280 in the British Library. Calendar illustrations were a speciality and these he seems often to have painted for manuscripts in which the larger miniatures were executed by other leading illuminators of the day, including Simon Marmion (*d.* 1489) and the Prayerbook Master of *c.* 1500. Illustrations in a few secular books have also been attributed to him. The illustrations in the Isabella Breviary must certainly be regarded as the masterpieces of his style, both for the ambitious scale of the work and for the striking originality of its content. There are however noticeable variations in the quality and in the finer points of style within the Breviary cycle and in the wider spectrum of work grouped under the name of this painter. This is not an appropriate place to attempt a detailed examination, but an illuminator of his undoubted standing can be expected to have attracted pupils and assistants who would have been employed alongside their master in a major commission of this kind.

The second largest contributor to the manuscript, completing the sequence of illustration to the Sanctorale, was the illuminator known as the Master of James IV of Scotland (fig. 55 onwards). Most of the miniatures which he painted for this manuscript

(*Left*) 28 Psalm 118, verse 33 (at Terce): Adam and Eve cast out of Paradise; the coming of the Holy Spirit at Pentecost (f. 177*v* detail).

(*Right*) 29 Psalm 126: God and his saints appearing above a newly built church (f. 186 detail).

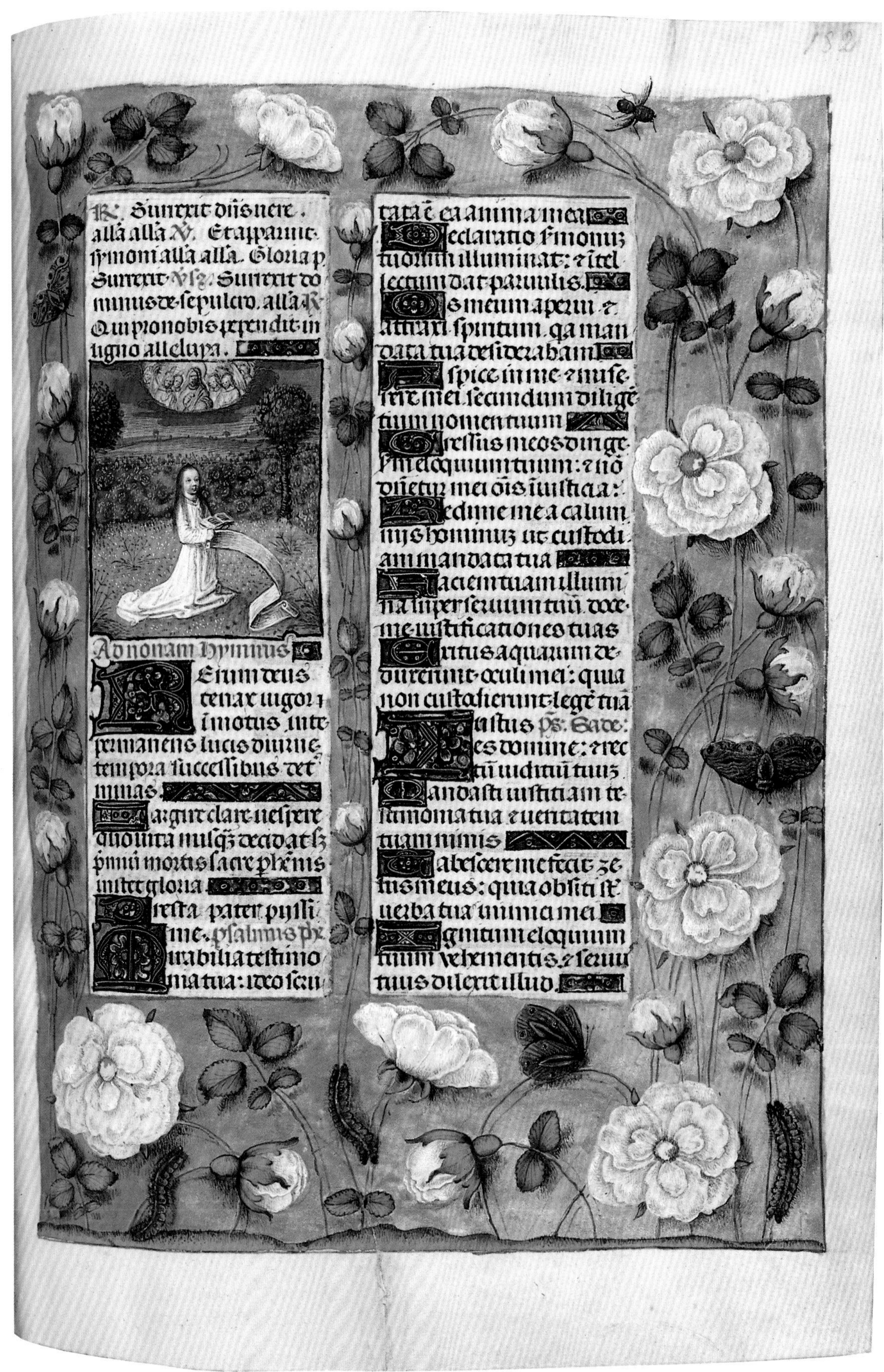

30 Psalm 118, verse 129 (at None): a suppliant in the mystic rose garden (f. 182).

31 Psalms 119–121: (*left*) to mark the beginning of the 15 gradual psalms, David and his musicians are shown ascending the symbolic 15 steps of the Temple; (*right*) Solomon overseeing the building of the Temple (ff. 184*v*–185).

are small pictures of individual saints, offering little scope for the display of narrative skills. Even the three large miniatures due to him, the Coronation of the Virgin (fig.2), All Saints (fig.65) and the Raising of Lazarus (fig.66), address subjects common to many of the liturgical manuscripts of the day. He thus enjoyed far less opportunity for originality and dramatic presentation than the Master of the Dresden Prayerbook and his work certainly seems calm and static by comparison. It is however particularly notable for the skill with which the colours and textures of fabrics are handled. The name of this artist is due to his appearance in a magnificent book of hours now in Vienna, which was made to celebrate the marriage of King James IV of Scotland to Margaret Tudor, elder daughter of Henry VII of England, in 1503. It is now widely held that he was in fact the celebrated Gerard Horenbout, subsequently court painter to Margaret of Austria. Horenbout's contribution to the Sforza Hours (British Library, Additional MS 34294) is documented in 1519 and he is also said to have been among the artists of the Grimani Breviary in Venice. He was born in Ghent about 1465 and became a master in the Bruges painters' guild in 1487. If he and the Master of James IV are indeed one and the same, then the miniatures in the Isabella Breviary are among his earliest securely dated works.

Four large miniatures within that part of the manuscript attributable to the Master of the Dresden Prayerbook are completely different in style from anything else in the book. Two, the Nativity (fig.7) and the Adoration of the Magi (fig.9), occur near the beginning of the Temporale and the others, St Barbara (fig.45) and St John the Evangelist (fig.46), near the beginning of the Sanctorale. It has long been recognised that the two scenes from the Christmas story are closely related to paintings by Gerard David. The Nativity reverses his treatment of the same subject which is now in the Metropolitan Museum of Art in New York, and the Adoration follows the panel in the Alte Pinacothek in Munich. The seated St Barbara is very much in the same tradition as other figures of female saints attributable to David. The St John may also echo panel painting, though there is no precise parallel. The inclusion of minute scenes from the Apocalypse is very reminiscent of the right-hand wing of the famous altarpiece which Hans Memling painted in 1479 for the Hospital of St John in Bruges.

Many commentators have held that the author of these four miniatures was Gerard David himself. Born at Oudewater in Holland about 1460, he was active in Bruges from 1484 and took over the leading position enjoyed by Memling when the older master, recorded as one of the richest citizens of the town, died in 1494. Although he can certainly be shown to have links with the professional illuminators working in Bruges, there is no documentary evidence to indicate that David himself ever undertook manuscript

(*Left*) 32 Psalm 143: David and Goliath (f.191*v* detail).

(*Right*) 33 The Canticle of the Three Children; Daniel III, 57: Shadrach, Meshach and Abednego cast into the fiery furnace (f.194*v* detail).

painting. The great differences of technique due to differences of medium make direct comparisons between the Isabella miniatures and his panels very difficult. A number of tiny devotional paintings for personal use are however attributed to him, and these are conceived on much the same scale as manuscript paintings. Close scrutiny of the four Isabella subjects alongside the work of other contributors to the Breviary does show up some quite distinct differences, particularly in the approach to the modelling of faces and hands. The two main artists, who are recognisably manuscript painters by profession, tend to achieve their results by applying sketchy linear outlines to particular features in a manner that is paralleled, though on a greatly exaggerated scale, by modern cartoonists. Seen under high magnification, their results often seem quite crude. By contrast, the 'David' faces and hands may be seen as built up gradually by means of countless tiny dabs of pigment applied with the point of a brush. This is quite similar to the method used to model features on the few drawings attributed to David and certainly suggests that the craftsman responsible was trained in a tradition different from that of his collaborators. This perhaps supports the idea that the artist was a panel painter, though not necessarily David himself.

In the body of the book, at the end of the portion connected with the Master of the Dresden Prayerbook but before the first of the miniatures by the Master of James IV, there is a hiatus of five quires (ff. 362–411) in which, although the decorative border work seems to belong to the same campaign as that in preceding quires, the miniatures were all supplied at later dates. Twelve illustrations were lacking from this area of the manuscript, five large and seven small. One of these, a large miniature of the murder of the Dominican St Peter Martyr (f. 365), was supplied by a more than somewhat inept

(*Left*) 34 The Athanasian Creed: a Pope and church dignitaries presiding over the burning of heretical books (f. 196*v* detail).

(*Right*) 35 The litany of saints: leaders of church and state, including a pope, an emperor and a king of France, supplicate Christ and his elect (f. 198 detail).

36 Easter Sunday: the Resurrection (f.211).

37 Pentecost: the Descent of the Holy Spirit (f.234).

38 Trinity Sunday: St Augustine confronting the child who compared his efforts to explain the mystery of the Trinity with the exercise of attempting to empty the sea into a little hole (f.241).

39 Trinity I: the parable of Dives and Lazarus; Luke XVI, 19–31 (f.252).

40 Saturday before the first Sunday in August: Solomon instructing his son; Proverbs 1 (f.260).

41 The first Sunday in September: the tribulations of Job (f. 262).

hand apparently soon after the manuscript was finished. At a similar date two small miniatures were added in the second unfinished quire, two large and a small in the fourth quire, and a single large one (the Visititation, fig. 54) in the fifth. All but the Peter Martyr scene are painted on separate pieces of vellum, trimmed to size and laid down in the empty spaces left for them. This may suggest that the book was already bound when they were commissioned, making it awkward and somewhat risky for a not very competent painter to work direct upon the page. As the existing binding apparently incorporates leather panels from a late 15th century Spanish cover, these additions may have been made in Spain.

The remaining five gaps persisted into the 19th century. In 1817 Dibdin drew attention to the lack of a large miniature of St Catherine of Siena, expressing a hope that 'Mr Dent . . . will get it supplied by a copy of some other clever figure, of the same character, executed about the same time.' The result appears at f. 368 (fig. 53) and the same hand supplied, within the same quire, small pictures of Sts George (f. 363*v*), Mark (f. 364), and Philip and James (f. 367). At the end of the third of the unfinished quires he also painted a representation of the Ten Thousand Martyrs (f. 385*v*). On the pages where these smaller subjects were lacking, the original artists had provided only the three-quarter borders normally associated with initials rather than the full borders standard for miniature pages, which may account for their neglect when the earlier additions were made.

The borders in the Isabella Breviary merit comment in their own right. They involve at least one noteworthy illuminator whose hand appears elsewhere undertaking independent commissions for books of hours. This painter contributed the borders surrounding the calendar pages (reproduced here on the title verso page), which enclose the usual scenes of the labours of the months, combined with signs of the zodiac. His distinctive, if not very polished, figure style reappears in several unusual borders associated with

(*Left*) 42 The third Sunday in September: the charitable acts of Tobit; Tobit 1 (f. 263*v* detail).
(*Right*) 43 The dedication of a church (f. 289 detail).

44 St Andrew (f.293).

45 St Barbara (f. 297).

46 St John the Evangelist (f. 309).

large miniatures by the Master of the Dresden Prayerbook (for example fig. 10) and the treatment of those figures alongside the Entry of Christ into Jerusalem (fig. 15), where they echo the action in the miniature, suggests very close collaboration between the two illuminators. He liked to combine woven branches, or a type of heavy strapwork reminiscent of document decoration (fig. 14), with the more usual elements of the late Flemish illusionistic border. Characteristic birds, which re-surface in a number of the more traditional border compositions in the first portion of the manuscript, suggest that he was involved in the execution of a majority of the marginal schemes associated with the miniatures of the Master of the Dresden Prayerbook. This group of borders extends as far as f. 411, after which the miniature cycle is taken over by the Master of James IV, and the borders, though many of them are superficially related closely to the traditional borders of the earlier pages, betray a subtly different, much smoother style of painting. Also at this point in the manuscript the earlier type of border of acanthus and flowers on plain vellum finally disappears, apart from an example associated with the opening miniature of the common of saints, painted by the first illuminator but as already noted, not necessarily executed at the end of the campaign on the manuscript.

SOME CONCLUSIONS

There seems no good reason to doubt that the manuscript was presented to Isabella of Castile, as the arms and dedicatory inscription suggest, to mark the double marriage of her children. This event in fact inspired numerous works of art, including portraits (fig. 3), manuscripts (figs 4, 5) and even an elaborate scheme of stained glass for a private chapel in Antwerp. The fact that there are no further marks of ownership in the book

(*Left*) 47 The massacre of the innocents (f. 312 detail).
(*Right*) 48 The conversion of St Paul (f. 328*v* detail).

49 St Thomas Aquinas with the crucifix that miraculously spoke to him (f.348).

need not be regarded as an obstacle. Both the other outstanding illuminated breviaries from Flemish workshops of the period, the Grimani Breviary in the library of St Mark's in Venice and the Mayer van den Bergh manuscript in Antwerp, are completely without evidence to identify a first owner. Isabella's taste for Flemish works of art is well attested and it was just at this time that she personally employed two Flemish painters, Michel Sittow, whose early career was associated with Bruges, and Juan de Flandes, who first appears in her accounts in 1496.

There seem to be clear indications that the manuscript did reach Spain before the end of the 15th century. The two leather panels of Mudéjar-style blind tooling incorporated into the current early 19th-century binding by Hering are certainly Spanish in origin. As we have already seen, the book is said to have been taken from the Escorial. Furthermore it would appear that the very rare miniature of the Temptations of Christ (fig. 11), painted in the manuscript by the Master of the Dresden Prayerbook, was the direct source for a tiny panel painting of the same subject executed by Juan de Flandes for Isabella and now in the National Gallery of Art in Washington. Two further miniatures from the Breviary, the entry into Jerusalem (fig. 15) and the Last Supper (fig. 16), are also reflected among the panels which the Flemish painter produced for his Spanish patroness.

The connection of de Rojas with such an outstanding Flemish book need occasion no surprise. Not only was he responsible for commissioning the elegant illumination of the two copies of the marriage treaty of 1495 now in Spain, but he was also himself portrayed on the wing of an altarpiece which has been attributed to Hans Memling. It is very likely that the splendid book of hours destined for Isabella and now in Cleveland was also acquired through him. This hours combines work by the Master of the Older Prayer-book of Maximilian, the Master of James IV of Scotland, the Master of the Prayerbooks of *c.* 1500 and the Master of the Dresden Prayerbook. From available reproductions it

(*Left*) 50 St Peter's Chair (f. 345*v* detail). (*Right*) 51 St Vincent Ferrer (f. 358 detail).

52 The Annunciation, flanking the Tree of Jesse (f. 354).

53 St Catherine of Siena, added by a 19th-century artist (f.368).

54 The Visitation, added by a hand of about 1500 (f.399).

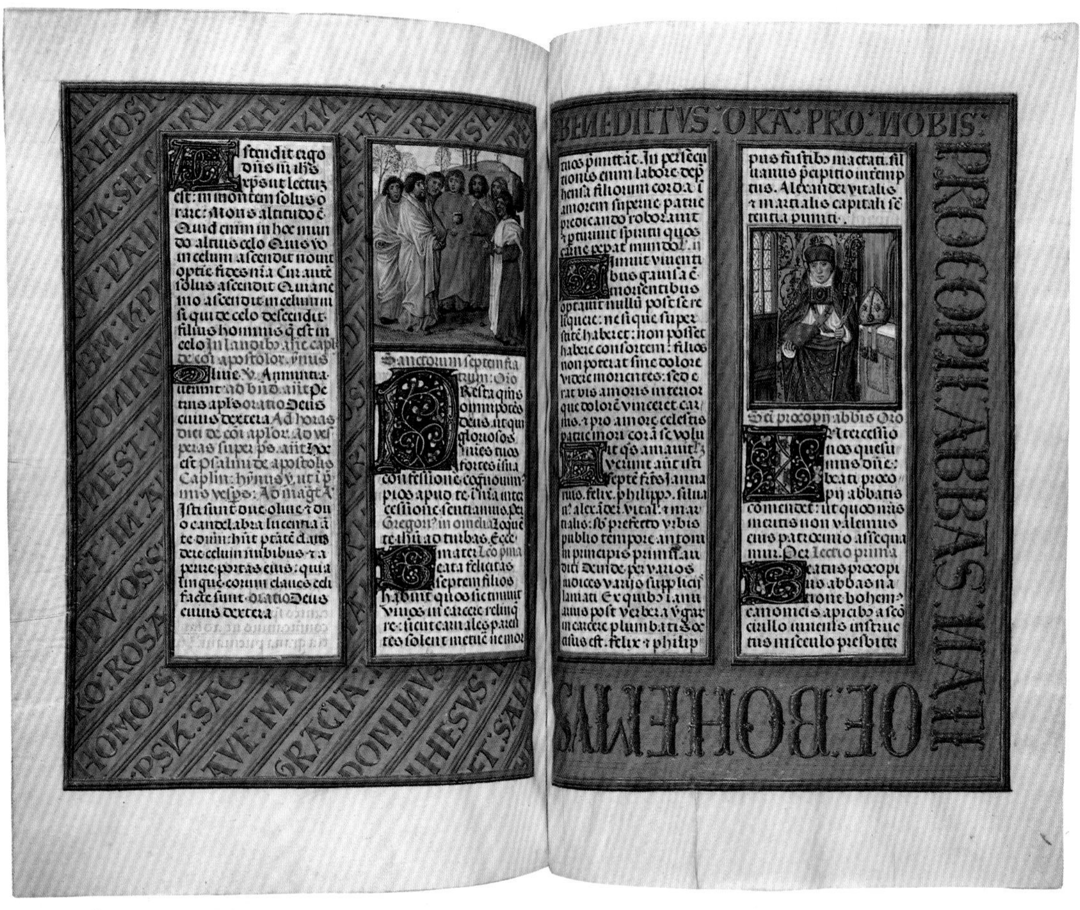

55 The Seven Brothers (*left*) and (*right*) St Procopius (ff.404*v*–405).

appears that the marriage treaties are also attributable to the Master of the Older Prayerbook of Maximilian. There is however no direct proof that de Rojas himself originally commissioned the breviary nor even that it was intended from the first for Isabella. The break in the execution of the illumination, marked by the added miniatures, and the change to a completely different artist thereafter might indicate that work on the book was for some reason halted before completion and only taken up again after a lapse of time. It could have been merely taken over by the ambassador of Ferdinand and Isabella, an earlier client having failed to carry through the project.

The Old Testament cycle decorating the psalter section of the breviary is the only likely source of clues to an alternative owner. Scenes from the life of David are of course the obvious theme for such a cycle. Not only was the author of the Psalms the direct ancestor of Christ, he was also regarded as a model of kingship. Within half a century of the production of this manuscript, both Henry VIII of England and Francis I of France had themselves recognisably portrayed as the Old Testament king in manuscripts written for their personal use. In this book however some very unusual scenes are portrayed, not all involving David, and it might be possible to interpret the emphasis on the destruction and rebuilding of Jerusalem and on rejoicings in the Temple with reference

(*Top left*) 56 St Appollinaris (f.411*v* detail). (*Right*) 57 St Anne teaching the Virgin to read (f.414 detail).
(*Bottom left*) 58 St Martha (f.417 detail). (*Right*) 59 St Peter's Chains (f.419*v* detail).

to the general awareness of the need for a new crusade. It is worth noting the miniature introducing the litany of the saints (fig.35), where the leaders of the Christian world are kneeling in supplication before the heavenly hosts. The group includes both the Pope and the Emperor, while the foreground figure with his back to the reader is wearing the blue robe powdered with fleurs-de-lys of a king of France. In 1493 the Peace of Senlis temporarily reconciled Maximilian with France and, after the death of his father, the Emperor Frederick III, in August of that year, Maximilian did make an ineffectual plea to the rulers of Europe to unite against the Turks. Within a few months, however, Maximilian had concluded an alliance with the Sforza Dukes of Milan and Charles VIII of France was preparing his forces for an invasion of Italy, directed at the conquest of the Kingdom of Naples but claimed as the first step towards a new Holy War. Early in 1495 he declared himself King of Sicily and Jerusalem, usurping one of Ferdinand's titles. The new situation greatly enhanced the desirability of the marriage treaties cementing relations between Maximilian and Spain, both anxious to provide firm opposition to the grandiose ambitions of France.

Of the several other liturgical manuscripts made for Isabella which have survived, two breviaries, now in Madrid and in the Escorial respectively, both follow the universally applicable Use of Rome rather than a local one. Both books were produced within Spain itself. Nevertheless Isabella does remain the prime candidate for association with the London breviary and its Dominican text is entirely appropriate to her. The Dominican Order had strong Spanish connections from its inception, for St Dominic was himself a native of Castile. The purpose of the Order was from the beginning to combat heresy

(*Left*) 60 St Dominic (f.423*v* detail). (*Right*) 61 St Bernard (f.441 detail).

and unbelief, from which identification with the Inquisition naturally developed. The Conquest of Granada and the expulsion or forced conversion of the Moorish and Jewish communities of Spain, however repugnant to 20th-century susceptibilities, were the background to some of the greatest triumphs in the Order's history. With these activities Isabella was closely identified. Several of the unusual subjects in the illustration of the manuscript apparently reflect the work of the Order. Most obvious is the miniature which introduces the creed (fig.34), where a Pope and leaders of the church are shown burning heretical books. A vision of the Passion and of sufferings of the martyrs hovers over David and his Jewish priestly cantors, who clutch the roses and lilies so often used allegorically in Christian art and writings to symbolise aspects of salvation (fig.22). The 'old song' gives place to the new as angels sing their traditional salute to Christ's birth (fig.24), and Abraham rescues his brother Lot from the evil forces of Sodom and is greeted by Melchisedek the priest, who offers him the bread and wine symbolic of the Mass (fig.25). In this latter scene the Holy Trinity is introduced in an unusual guise. God the Father, on the right, wears the traditional papal tiara and carries an orb, but God the Son is in full armour beneath a cloak, with a crowned helm and a sceptre. Between them they support, not the conventional dove representing the Holy Spirit, but a chalice and a copy of Holy Writ. The reference to the need for military force to be used in ensuring the purity and stability of the Christian faith, as at Granada in 1492, seems very clear.

Isabella was in fact very specifically associated, not only with the Grand Inquisitor Thomas de Torquemada himself, but also with the Dominican house established at Avila

(*Left*) 62 St John the Baptist (f.449 detail). (*Right*) 63 The birth of the Virgin (f.451*v* detail).

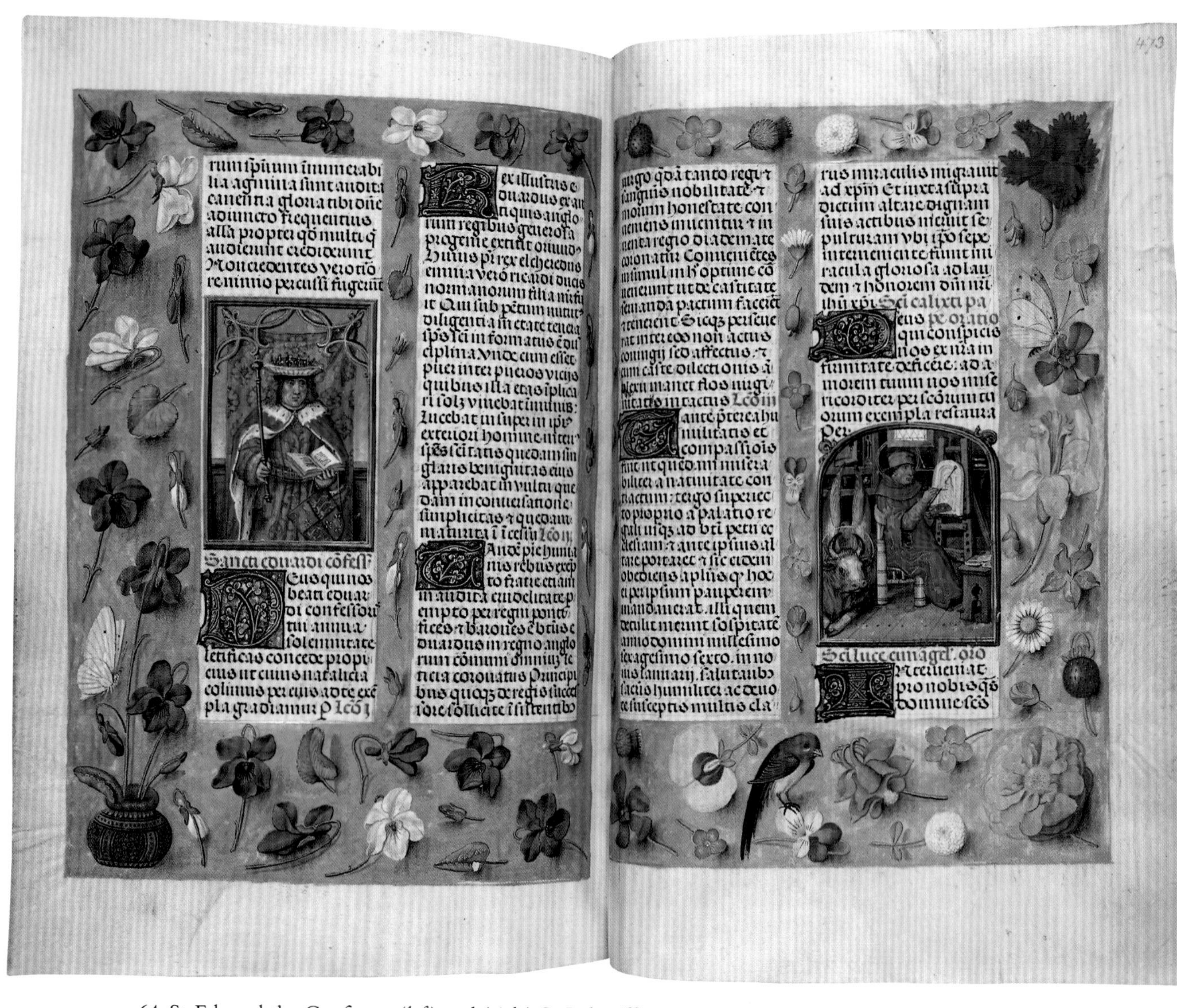

64 St Edward the Confessor (*left*) and (*right*) St Luke (ff.472*v*–473).

under his direction. Founded shortly before 1480 and dedicated to Torquemada's own patron, St Thomas Aquinas, it was largely financed through royal patronage with monies seized from the Jews and Moors who had fled into exile. Here, as in many other ecclesiastical buildings raised during the last two decades of the 15th century, the arms and badges of 'los Reyes Católicos' feature in decoration throughout the complex. They are also prominent in the community's richly illuminated choir books, today known only from shattered fragments. A painting now in the Prado in Madrid was originally designed for Avila. It shows Ferdinand and Isabella with two of their children presented to the Virgin and Child by saints of the Dominican Order. To the right Isabella and an Infanta (possibly Joanna, if the painting is, as seems likely, later than the marriage of the Infanta Isabella to the Crown Prince of Portugal in 1490) are supported by St Dominic himself and by a lesser figure identifiable as St Peter Martyr. On the left Ferdinand and the Infante John are accompanied by St Thomas Aquinas, who is carrying a model of

65 All Saints (f.477*v*).

the church, and by a second friar who has been called Torquemada but who may equally well be a fourth Dominican saint, Vincent Ferrer.

The Avila house was finished by 1493. As early as the following year the Borgia Pope Alexander VI, endeavouring to relax Torquemada's stranglehold on the Inquisition in Spain without losing the support of Ferdinand and Isabella (to whom he diplomatically awarded the title 'los Reyes Católicos' in 1495 at the height of the French threat to Italy), was suggesting that the Grand Inquisitor might care to retire to the Castilian community to conserve his health. Two years later he in fact did so, and was buried there when he died in 1498. The presence of her old friend and adviser must have strengthened Isabella's own links with the community. But even stronger evidence of her personal connection with the Dominican house at Avila is the fact that it was chosen as the resting place of her only son and heir, the Infante John, whose body was conveyed there from Salamanca, amidst the most elaborate manifestations of grief, in the late autumn of 1497. A magnificent Renaissance tomb now marks his grave.

The appearance of the arms of her two children and their spouses alongside the arms of Isabella and her husband on the dedicatory opening of the Isabella Breviary suggests that the gift of the book must date from before John's much-lamented death. It is unlikely that it was offered before the conclusion of the formal marriage agreements early in 1495, perhaps even before the proxy weddings had taken place in the November of that year. It would be nice to think that it was conveyed by de Rojas himself, when he accompanied Margaret of Austria to Spain at the beginning of 1497, though traffic between Flanders and Spain must have been frequent throughout the relevant period. The manuscript itself must surely have been commissioned well in advance of its presentation, for such a complex scheme of decoration would probably have taken several years to complete.

It is astonishing that so famous and so rich a book has until now been so little studied. A substantial number even of its most ambitious and unusual miniatures have never before been published. Much more remains to be revealed by future investigation.

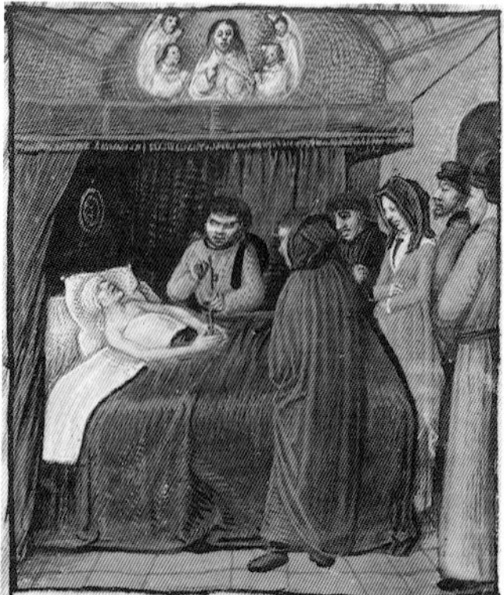

The Canticle of Simeon; Luke II, 29–32: deathbed scene (f. 196 detail).

SUMMARY DESCRIPTION OF THE MANUSCRIPT

BRITISH LIBRARY ADDITIONAL MS 18851

Vellum; 523 leaves + one un-numbered blank (now f.7*). Approximately 230 × 160 mm. Written in a rounded gothic script in two columns, 34 lines to the page. Early 19th-century binding of blind-tooled dark brown morocco with doublures, according to Dibdin by Charles Hering, with panels of blind-tooled Mudéjar decoration, apparently from an earlier cover, laid down on both front and back boards. Contained in a box covered with blind-tooled Russia, lined with crimson silk velvet, presumably also by Hering.

The following is a list of the miniatures not reproduced here. All are small unless otherwise stated:

(1) In the calendar: borders representing the labours of the months and signs of the zodiac, ff. 1*v*–7.

(2) In the first portion of the Temporale: Advent I: the day of wrath (f. 14*v*); Advent III: John the Baptist in prison and the beginning of the ministry of Christ (f. 18); Advent IV: the baptism of Christ (f. 23); Sexagesima: Noah's Ark (f. 65*v*); Quinquagesima: Abraham and his family commanded to set out for the Promised Land (f. 67*v*); Lent II (large): the woman of Canaan pleading with Christ to cast out the devil from her daughter (f. 77); Good Friday: twelve further scenes from the story of the Passion (ff. 100*v*–102, 103*v*–104); Good Friday (large): the Crucifixion (f. 106*v*); Holy Saturday: soldiers sleeping around Christ's tomb (f. 108*v*).

(3) In the psalter etc.: Psalm 114: David taking the cup and spear from the tent of Saul (f. 174*v*); Psalm 118, verse 81 (at Sext): Jacob's ladder (f. 180); Psalm 131: the arrival of the Ark greeted with music and sacrifice (f. 187); Psalm 137: Goliath issuing his challenge (f. 189); 'Te deum': baptism of a male saint (f. 194); 'Magnificat': the Visitation (f. 195*v*).

(4) At the rubric concerning readings from the gospels: a Dominican superior reading to his community (f. 203).

(5) In the second portion of the Temporale: readings from the Apocalypse during Easter: St John on Patmos (f. 220*v*); the Ascension (large): Christ disappearing into heaven (f. 228); the first Sunday in October: Alexander slaying Darius (f. 266); the first Sunday in November: a congregation at prayer within a chapel (f. 270).

(6) In the Sanctorale: the Coronation of the Virgin (f. 301); Lucy (f. 303); Thomas the Apostle (f. 304*v*); Stephen (f. 306); Thomas Becket (f. 314*v*); Anthony Abbot (f. 320*v*); Fabian and Sebastian (f. 322*v*); Agnes (f. 324); Vincent (f. 326); translation of Thomas Aquinas (f. 331*v*); the Presentation (large, f. 337); Matthias (f. 347); George (19th cent., f. 363*v*); Mark (19th cent., f. 364); Peter Martyr (large, add. *c.* 1500, f. 365); Philip and James (19th cent., f. 367); the Invention of the Cross (add. *c.* 1500, f. 372); Christ crowned with thorns (add. *c.* 1500, f. 374); 10000 Martyrs (19th cent., f. 385*v*); the birth of the Baptist (large, add. *c.* 1500, f. 386*v*); John and Paul (add. *c.* 1500, f. 390); decollation of Peter and Paul (large, add. *c.* 1500, f. 392); Alexius (f. 405*v*); Margaret (f. 406*v*); Praxedis (f. 407*v*); Mary Magdalene (f. 408); James the Great (f. 412*v*); Felix, Simplicius, Faustinus and Beatrice (f. 418); the Invention of Stephen (f. 421*v*); the Transfiguration (f. 427); Lawrence (f. 431); Bartholomew (f. 442*v*); Louis IX (f. 444); Augustine (f. 445*v*); Gorgonius, Prothus and Hyacinthus, and the

66 Office of the Dead: the raising of Lazarus (f.481).

(*Top left*) 67 The 11,000 Virgins (f.474*v* detail). (*Right*) 68 St Martin (f.485*v* detail).
(*Bottom left*) 69 St Cecilia (f.491*v* detail). (*Right*) 70 St Clement (f.494 detail).

Exaltation of the Cross (combined into one large miniature, f.455); Euphemia (f.458); Matthew (f.459); Maurice and his companions (f.461); Cosmas and Damian (f.462); Wenceslas (f.463*v*); Michael (f.464); Jerome (f.467*v*); Remigius (f.468*v*); Francis (f.469*v*); Pope Marcus (f.470*v*); Denis and his companions (f.471); Simon and Jude (f.476); the Four Crowned Martyrs (f.484*v*); Theodore (f.485); Elizabeth (f.488*v*); Catherine (f.495*v*).

(7) At the common of saints: the Apostles (f.499).

FURTHER READING

References to earlier literature on the manuscript will be found in *Renaissance Painting in Manuscripts: Treasures from the British Library,* ed. T. Kren, New York 1983, no.5 and in H.J. Van Miegroet, *Gerard David,* Antwerp 1989, no.85. The latter summarises opinions about the miniatures attributed to David. Other works attributed to the principal artists of the Isabella Breviary are listed in G. Dogaer, *Flemish Miniature Painting in the 15th and 16th Centuries,* Amsterdam 1987. M. Evans, *The Sforza Hours,* London, The British Library 1992, discusses the later works of Horenbout.

For the general background to the period see W. Prevenier and W. Blockmans, *The Burgundian Netherlands,* Cambridge 1986 and the exhibition catalogue *Circa 1492: Art in the Age of Exploration,* ed. J. A. Levenson, National Gallery of Art, Washington 1991 (especially the articles by J. Brown, 'Spain in the age of exploration: crossroads of artistic culture', pp.41–9, and R. L. Kagan, 'The Spain of Ferdinand and Isabella', pp.55–61). The Juan de Flandes panel of the Temptations of Christ is reproduced in colour in *Circa 1492,* p.163; on this see further J. O. Hand and M. Wolff, *Early Netherlandish Painting,* National Gallery of Art, Washington 1986, pp.123–39. The Duke of Alba's copy of the marriage treaty is reproduced in H. d'Hulst, *Le Mariage de Philippe le Beau avec Jeanne de Castile à Lierre le 20 Octobre 1496,* Antwerp 1958, frontispiece and p.16. For the panel of Ferdinand and Isabella and their children with Dominican saints, in colour, see the exhibition catalogue *Hispania Austria: I Re Cattolici, Massimiliano I e gli Inizi della Casa d'Austria in Spagna,* Milan 1992, p.107.

For the liturgical contents of the Dominican breviary see A. A. King, *Liturgies of the Religious Orders,* London 1955, chapter 5.

For other manuscripts owned by Isabella see the exhibition catalogue *Les Rois Bibliophiles,* ed. A. Sarriá, Bibliothèque Royale Albert Ier, Brussels 1985, chapter III, and P. M. de Winter, 'A Book of Hours of Queen Isabel la Católica', *Bulletin of the Cleveland Museum of Art,* 1981, pp.342–427.

Many books, of extremely variable quality, have been written about the life and times of Ferdinand and Isabella. It is still interesting to peruse two major publications, both by American authors, which appeared in England while the Isabella Breviary was still in private hands: W. H. Prescott, *A History of the Reign of Ferdinand and Isabella the Catholic* (3 vols.), 1838 and Washington Irving, *A Chronicle of the Conquest of Granada* (2 vols.), 1829. Both have been many times reprinted.